T0015137

PEREGRINE FALCON VS. RED-TAILED HAWK

BY NATHAN SOMMER

BELLWETHER MEDIA • MINNEAPOLIS, MN

Torque brims with excitement
perfect for thrill-seekers of all kinds.
Discover daring survival skills, explore
uncharted worlds, and marvel at mighty
engines and extreme sports. In *Torque* books,
anything can happen. Are you ready?

This edition first published in 2024 by Bellwether Media, Inc.

No part of this publication may be reproduced in whole or in part without written
permission of the publisher. For information regarding permission, write to
Bellwether Media, Inc., Attention: Permissions Department,
6012 Blue Circle Drive, Minnetonka, MN 55343.

Library of Congress Cataloging-in-Publication Data

LC record for Peregrine Falcon vs. Red-tailed Hawk available at:
https://lccn.loc.gov/2023042542

Text copyright © 2024 by Bellwether Media, Inc. TORQUE and associated logos are
trademarks and/or registered trademarks of Bellwether Media, Inc.

Editor: Suzane Nguyen   Designer: Josh Brink

Printed in the United States of America, North Mankato, MN.

TABLE OF CONTENTS

THE COMPETITORS

Raptors are fearsome **predators** with amazing attack abilities! Among them, peregrine falcons are the fastest. They use speed to take out **prey** in the air.

Red-tailed hawks challenge peregrine falcons for control of the sky. These large birds swoop toward their prey. They quickly strike animals on the ground. Who would win in a battle of the birds?

Peregrine falcons are some of the most widespread birds of prey. They are found on every **continent** except Antarctica. They live in open **habitats** near water. The birds often nest on high places like cliffs and skyscrapers.

These falcons have bluish-gray bodies with white necks and underbellies. Yellow circles surround their dark eyes.

LIFE PARTNERS

Peregrine falcons often have young with the same partner for life.

PEREGRINE FALCON PROFILE

```
0          1          2          3          4
FOOT      FEET       FEET       FEET
```

WINGSPAN
UP TO 3.6 FEET
(1.1 METERS)

HEIGHT
UP TO 1.6 FEET
(0.5 METERS)

WEIGHT
UP TO 3.5 POUNDS
(1.6 KILOGRAMS)

HABITAT

MOUNTAINS   TUNDRA   DESERTS   FORESTS

PEREGRINE FALCON RANGE

☐ RANGE

RED-TAILED HAWK PROFILE

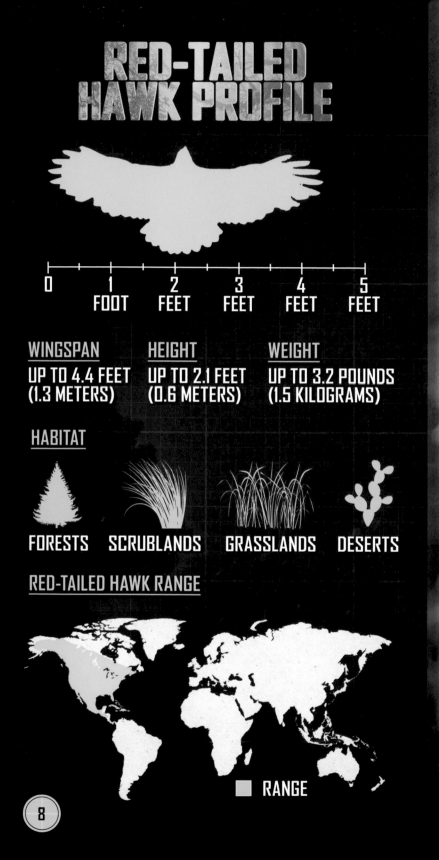

```
0       1       2       3       4       5
      FOOT    FEET    FEET    FEET    FEET
```

WINGSPAN
UP TO 4.4 FEET
(1.3 METERS)

HEIGHT
UP TO 2.1 FEET
(0.6 METERS)

WEIGHT
UP TO 3.2 POUNDS
(1.5 KILOGRAMS)

HABITAT

FORESTS   SCRUBLANDS   GRASSLANDS   DESERTS

RED-TAILED HAWK RANGE

■ RANGE

Red-tailed hawks are some of North America's largest hawks. Their wingspans reach up to 4.4 feet (1.3 meters) wide. They have broad, rounded wings and thick bodies.

Red-tailed hawks are found throughout much of North and Central America. The hawks are often found in open places like grasslands and roadsides. They easily spot prey there.

SECRET WEAPONS

Peregrine falcons have powerful eyes. The falcons use one eye to find animals from far away. They use both eyes when they spot prey up close.

Red-tailed hawks also have super eyesight! The hawks use their eyesight to find small prey from up in the sky. They can spot tiny mice from 100 feet (30 meters) above the ground!

SUPER SIGHT

Both peregrine falcons and red-tailed hawks have eyesight that is eight times stronger than a human's eyesight!

UP TO 238 MILES (383 KILOMETERS) PER HOUR

PEREGRINE FALCON

UP TO 70 MILES (113 KILOMETERS) PER HOUR

CHEETAH

Peregrine falcons are the world's fastest animals. Long, pointed wings help them dive fast. They can reach up to 238 miles (383 kilometers) per hour. Prey often do not see them coming!

Red-tailed hawks are built to **soar**. Their broad, rounded wings allow them to hover in strong winds. This helps them cover more hunting ground.

SECRET WEAPONS

EYESIGHT | SPEED | SHARP TALONS

Peregrine falcons close their feet to deliver fast and deadly blows. Then they use their sharp **talons** to defeat prey. Their talons hold on to prey and cut through feathers.

SECRET WEAPONS

EYESIGHT   **ROUNDED WINGS**   **CURVED TALONS**

RED-TAILED HAWK TALON SIZE

**1.3 INCHES
(3.3 CENTIMETERS)**

Red-tailed hawks have sharp, curved talons. Their talons grow up to 1.3 inches (3.3 centimeters) long. These help the birds grab prey from the ground.

ATTACK MOVES

Peregrine falcons mostly hunt birds. From high up, they use their great eyesight to spot birds below. The falcons quickly dive toward prey once they spot it.

HUNTING PARTNERS

Humans have trained peregrine falcons to hunt for them for thousands of years.

Red-tailed hawks mainly hunt small **mammals**. They fly slowly in circles or **perch** to watch for prey. The birds swoop down quickly to attack!

Peregrine falcons slam into prey with closed feet. This can stun and defeat most prey. The falcons use their talons to capture smaller birds in midair!

Red-tailed hawks are very strong. They can carry animals that weigh up to 5 pounds (2.3 kilograms)!

Red-tailed hawks catch prey with their sharp talons. The hawks squeeze their prey tightly to defeat it. Then they pull their meal apart with their beaks.

READY, FIGHT!

A red-tailed hawk soars in the sky. It spots a mouse and swoops down to grab it. Suddenly, a peregrine falcon rams into the hawk!

The hawk cuts the falcon with its sharp talons. But the falcon flies up to slam into the hawk again. This time, the blow is deadly. The hawk was not quick enough for the speedy falcon today!

GLOSSARY

continent—one of the seven great divisions of land found on the globe

habitats—the homes or areas where animals prefer to live

mammals—warm-blooded animals that have backbones and feed their young milk

perch—to sit in a high place

predators—animals that hunt other animals for food

prey—animals that are hunted by other animals for food

raptors—large birds that hunt other animals; raptors are also called birds of prey.

soar—to fly without flapping wings

talons—sharp claws on birds that allow them to grab and tear into prey

TO LEARN MORE

AT THE LIBRARY

Lukidis, Lydia. *Falcons*. Mankato, Minn.: Black Rabbit Books, 2023.

Riggs, Kate. *Hawks*. Mankato, Minn.: Creative Education, 2022.

Sommer, Nathan. *Golden Eagle vs. Great Horned Owl*. Minneapolis, Minn.: Bellwether Media, 2021.

ON THE WEB

FACTSURFER

Factsurfer.com gives you a safe, fun way to find more information.

1. Go to www.factsurfer.com

2. Enter "peregrine falcon vs. red-tailed hawk" into the search box and click 🔍.

3. Select your book cover to see a list of related content.

INDEX

The images in this book are reproduced through the courtesy of: slowmotiongli, front cover (peregrine falcon); Arsgera, cover (red-tailed hawk); Harry Collins, pp. 2-3, 16, 20-24 (peregrine falcon head); Don Mammoser, pp. 2-3, 20-24 (peregrine falcon body); davidhoffmann photography, pp. 2-3, 20-24 (red-tailed hawk body); Jack FotoVerse, pp. 2-3, 20-24 (red-tailed hawk face); Harry Collins Photography, pp. 4, 14 (speed), 15 (eyesight); Ian Duffield, pp. 5, 17; Ken Griffiths, pp. 6-7; Stanislav Duben, pp. 8-9; Leena Robinson, p. 10; Brian E Kushner, p. 11; PixLove, p. 12; Keneva Photography, p. 13; Michael coulthurst, p. 14 (eyesight); Sriram Bird Photographer, p. 14 (sharp talons); StockPhotoAstur, p. 14; Todd Maertz, p. 15 (rounded wings); David Brace, p. 15 (curved talons); Rob Palmer Photography, p. 15; blickwinkel/ Alamy, p. 18; Tathoms, p. 19.